ILLUMINATE-YOUR-OWN GOSPEL OF MARK

FOR BIBLE JOURNALERS AND OTHERS WHO PRAY WITH A PEN

Edited by
GARY NEAL HANSEN

Climacus Publishing

For Dawna

And with special thanks to my dear friend Jack Craft for his generous support and encouragement.

PREFACE

A prayer that I love in the *Book of Common Prayer* asks God's help in getting the most out of the Scriptures. We pray that we might be able to "hear them, read, mark, learn, and inwardly digest them."

The *Illuminate-Your-Own Gospel of Mark* is a tool to help you see that prayer answered — especially by letting you quite literally "mark" the text of the Bible.

My inspiration in developing this project has been the scribes in medieval monasteries who spent long hours in the Word, copying out whole Bibles by hand. The most creative among them drew and wrote in the margins. Some produced masterpieces like the famous *Book of Kells*. Others made more casual doodles in the blank spaces. And still others left behind their thoughts in words around the text and between the lines.

I think they were onto something very useful: If you write in your Bible while you read, study, and pray, you'll have a richer encounter with the text — and you'll go deeper with God.

I wanted to make that easy for you. Instead of the usual uninterrupted block of text, I've divided the book into very small units, each two-page spread holding just one story or teaching. And the text is a generally unfamiliar translation — the *World English Bible* — so you can see each passage with fresh eyes.

You'll find lots of blank space, always including the full left-hand page. That leaves you plenty of room to fill up with your pens, colored pencils, or markers.

You can do what you want with those spaces, but I have several suggestions:

1. Draw all or part of what you see in the Gospel stories — people, places, or objects in a scene, or the little details of parables. It can help you listen for the meaning more carefully.

2. Draw pictures representing some part of your life that the text leads you to think about. It doesn't have to be fancy or artistic. What helps is expressing your prayer in a way that goes deeper than words.

3. Doodle decorations around the text as you listen to the words and pray through them. Many people find having something to do with their hands allows their minds to focus.

4. In the mode of an InterVarsity "Manuscript Study," mark up the text itself in colors and shapes. Circle all the names, underline all the verbs, color differently what is praised and why, and what is criticized and why —or whatever suits you. Ask questions of the text and dig for answers in the details.

5. When something in the text is difficult, write out your questions.
6. When the text reminds you to pray for someone, write down the prayer.
7. Once you've grappled with the text on the right, fill the left page like a regular journal, writing about what you read in the text and how it relates to your life.

You can use the *Illuminate-Your-Own Gospel of Mark* in any number of contexts.

- You can use it in your personal devotions.
- If your church has a sermon series on Mark (that's "Year B" in churches that use the lectionary) your child could use a copy during worship to draw about the sermon text — which means being focused on what matters.
- Grown ups could use a copy during sermons for the same reason!
- If your Bible study group is tired of study guides that ask simplistic questions and make you fill-in-the-blanks, try having each person draw and journal on each week's text in their copy of the *Illuminate-Your-Own Gospel of Mark*. Then at your group meeting, share what you drew and wrote, and dig in further with colored pencils.

The whole process is designed to let you bring more of yourself to Scripture, and therefore to draw closer to God. After all, God speaks to you through your imagination, your creativity, and your art just as much as through cool-headed academic study.

Go ahead. Mark God's Word. Pray with a pen. It's good for you.

I'll be praying for you!

Gary Neal Hansen

CHAPTER ONE

¹The beginning of the Good News of Jesus Christ, the
Son of God. ²As it is written in the prophets,

"Behold, I send my messenger before your face,
who will prepare your way before you:
³the voice of one crying in the wilderness,
'Make ready the way of the Lord!
Make his paths straight!'"

1:4 JOHN came baptizing in the wilderness and preaching the baptism of repentance for forgiveness of sins. ⁵All the country of Judea and all those of Jerusalem went out to him. They were baptized by him in the Jordan river, confessing their sins. ⁷John was clothed with camel's hair and a leather belt around his waist. He ate locusts and wild honey. ⁷He preached, saying, "After me comes he who is mightier than I, the thong of whose sandals I am not worthy to stoop down and loosen. ⁸I baptized you in water, but he will baptize you in the Holy Spirit."

1:9 IN THOSE DAYS, Jesus came from Nazareth of Galilee, and was baptized by John in the Jordan. ¹⁰Immediately coming up from the water, he saw the heavens parting, and the Spirit descending on him like a dove. ¹¹A voice came out of the sky, "You are my beloved Son, in whom I am well pleased."

1:12 IMMEDIATELY the Spirit drove him out into the wilderness. ¹³He was there in the wilderness forty days tempted by Satan. He was with the wild animals; and the angels were serving him.

1:14 Now AFTER John was taken into custody, Jesus came into Galilee, preaching the Good News of God's Kingdom, ¹⁵and saying, "The time is fulfilled, and God's Kingdom is at hand! Repent, and believe in the Good News."

1:16 PASSING ALONG by the sea of Galilee, he saw Simon and Andrew, the brother of Simon, casting a net into the sea, for they were fishermen. [17]Jesus said to them, "Come after me, and I will make you into fishers for men."

[18]Immediately they left their nets, and followed him.

1:19 GOING on a little further from there, he saw James the son of Zebedee, and John, his brother, who were also in the boat mending the nets. [20]Immediately he called them, and they left their father, Zebedee, in the boat with the hired servants, and went after him.

1:21 THEY went into Capernaum, and immediately on the Sabbath day he entered into the synagogue and taught. ²²They were astonished at his teaching, for he taught them as having authority, and not as the scribes. ²³Immediately there was in their synagogue a man with an unclean spirit, and he cried out, ²⁴saying, "Ha! What do we have to do with you, Jesus, you Nazarene? Have you come to destroy us? I know you who you are: the Holy One of God!"

²⁵Jesus rebuked him, saying, "Be quiet, and come out of him!"

²⁶The unclean spirit, convulsing him and crying with a loud voice, came out of him. ²⁷They were all amazed, so that they questioned among themselves, saying, "What is this? A new teaching? For with authority he commands even the unclean spirits, and they obey him!" ²⁸The report of him went out immediately everywhere into all the region of Galilee and its surrounding area.

1:29 IMMEDIATELY, when they had come out of the synagogue, they came into the house of Simon and Andrew, with James and John. ³⁰Now Simon's wife's mother lay sick with a fever, and immediately they told him about her. ³¹He came and took her by the hand, and raised her up. The fever left her immediately, and she served them. ³²At evening, when the sun had set, they brought to him all who were sick, and those who were possessed by demons. ³³All the city was gathered together at the door. ³⁴He healed many who were sick with various diseases, and cast out many demons. He didn't allow the demons to speak, because they knew him.

1:35 EARLY in the morning, while it was still dark, he rose up and went out, and departed into a deserted place, and prayed there.

1:36 Simon and those who were with him searched for him. [37]They found him and told him, "Everyone is looking for you."

[38]He said to them, "Let's go elsewhere into the next towns, that I may preach there also, because I came out for this reason." [39]He went into their synagogues throughout all Galilee, preaching and casting out demons.

1:40 A leper came to him, begging him, kneeling down to him, and saying to him, "If you want to, you can make me clean."

[41]Being moved with compassion, he stretched out his hand, and touched him, and said to him, "I want to. Be made clean." [42]When he had said this, immediately the leprosy departed from him, and he was made clean. [43]He strictly warned him, and immediately sent him out, [44]and said to him, "See you say nothing to anybody, but go show yourself to the priest, and offer for your cleansing the things which Moses commanded, for a testimony to them."

[45]But he went out, and began to proclaim it much, and to spread about the matter, so that Jesus could no more openly enter into a city, but was outside in desert places. People came to him from everywhere.

CHAPTER TWO

¹When he entered again into Capernaum after some days, it was heard that he was in the house. ²Immediately many were gathered together, so that there was no more room, not even around the door; and he spoke the word to them. ³Four people came, carrying a paralytic to him. ⁴When they could not come near to him for the crowd, they removed the roof where he was. When they had broken it up, they let down the mat that the paralytic was lying on. ⁵Jesus, seeing their faith, said to the paralytic, "Son, your sins are forgiven you."

⁶But there were some of the scribes sitting there, and reasoning in their hearts, ⁷"Why does this man speak blasphemies like that? Who can forgive sins but God alone?"

⁸Immediately Jesus, perceiving in his spirit that they so reasoned within themselves, said to them, "Why do you reason these things in your hearts? ⁹Which is easier, to tell the paralytic, 'Your sins are forgiven;' or to say, 'Arise, and take up your bed, and walk?' ¹⁰But that you may know that the Son of Man has authority on earth to forgive sins"—he said to the paralytic— ¹¹"I tell you, arise, take up your mat, and go to your house."

¹²He arose, and immediately took up the mat, and went out in front of them all; so that they were all amazed, and glorified God, saying, "We never saw anything like this!"

2:13 He went out again by the seaside. All the multitude came to him, and he taught them. [14]As he passed by, he saw Levi, the son of Alphaeus, sitting at the tax office, and he said to him, "Follow me." And he arose and followed him.

2:15 HE was reclining at the table in his house, and many tax collectors and sinners sat down with Jesus and his disciples, for there were many, and they followed him. ¹⁶The scribes and the Pharisees, when they saw that he was eating with the sinners and tax collectors, said to his disciples, "Why is it that he eats and drinks with tax collectors and sinners?"

¹⁷When Jesus heard it, he said to them, "Those who are healthy have no need for a physician, but those who are sick. I came not to call the righteous, but sinners to repentance."

2:18 JOHN's disciples and the Pharisees were fasting, and they came and asked him, "Why do John's disciples and the disciples of the Pharisees fast, but your disciples don't fast?"

[19]Jesus said to them, "Can the groomsmen fast while the bridegroom is with them? As long as they have the bridegroom with them, they can't fast. [20]But the days will come when the bridegroom will be taken away from them, and then they will fast in that day. [21]No one sews a piece of unshrunk cloth on an old garment, or else the patch shrinks and the new tears away from the old, and a worse hole is made. [22]No one puts new wine into old wineskins, or else the new wine will burst the skins, and the wine pours out, and the skins will be destroyed; but they put new wine into fresh wineskins."

2:23 HE was going on the Sabbath day through the grain fields, and his disciples began, as they went, to pluck the ears of grain. ²⁴The Pharisees said to him, "Behold, why do they do that which is not lawful on the Sabbath day?"

²⁵He said to them, "Did you never read what David did, when he had need, and was hungry—he, and those who were with him? ²⁶How he entered into God's house at the time of Abiathar the high priest, and ate the show bread, which is not lawful to eat except for the priests, and gave also to those who were with him?" ²⁷He said to them, "The Sabbath was made for man, not man for the Sabbath. ²⁸Therefore the Son of Man is lord even of the Sabbath."

CHAPTER THREE

¹He entered again into the synagogue, and there was a man there who had his hand withered. ²They watched him, whether he would heal him on the Sabbath day, that they might accuse him. ³He said to the man who had his hand withered, "Stand up." ⁴He said to them, "Is it lawful on the Sabbath day to do good, or to do harm? To save a life, or to kill?" But they were silent. ⁵When he had looked around at them with anger, being grieved at the hardening of their hearts, he said to the man, "Stretch out your hand." He stretched it out, and his hand was restored as healthy as the other. ⁶The Pharisees went out, and immediately conspired with the Herodians against him, how they might destroy him.

3:7 JESUS withdrew to the sea with his disciples, and a great multitude followed him from Galilee, from Judea, [8]from Jerusalem, from Idumaea, beyond the Jordan, and those from around Tyre and Sidon. A great multitude, hearing what great things he did, came to him. [9]He spoke to his disciples that a little boat should stay near him because of the crowd, so that they wouldn't press on him. [10]For he had healed many, so that as many as had diseases pressed on him that they might touch him. [11]The unclean spirits, whenever they saw him, fell down before him, and cried, "You are the Son of God!" [12]He sternly warned them that they should not make him known.

3:13 H<small>E</small> went up into the mountain, and called to himself those whom he wanted, and they went to him. ¹⁴He appointed twelve, that they might be with him, and that he might send them out to preach, ¹⁵and to have authority to heal sicknesses and to cast out demons: ¹⁶Simon (to whom he gave the name Peter); ¹⁷James the son of Zebedee; and John, the brother of James, (whom he called Boanerges, which means, Sons of Thunder); ¹⁸Andrew; Philip; Bartholomew; Matthew; Thomas; James, the son of Alphaeus; Thaddaeus; Simon the Zealot; ¹⁹and Judas Iscariot, who also betrayed him.

3:19 THEN HE came into a house. ²⁰The multitude came together again, so that they could not so much as eat bread. ²¹When his friends heard it, they went out to seize him; for they said, "He is insane." ²²The scribes who came down from Jerusalem said, "He has Beelzebul," and, "By the prince of the demons he casts out the demons."

²³He summoned them, and said to them in parables, "How can Satan cast out Satan? ²⁴ If a kingdom is divided against itself, that kingdom cannot stand. ²⁵If a house is divided against itself, that house cannot stand. ²⁶If Satan has risen up against himself, and is divided, he can't stand, but has an end. ²⁷But no one can enter into the house of the strong man to plunder unless he first binds the strong man; then he will plunder his house. ²⁸Most certainly I tell you, all sins of the descendants of man will be forgiven, including their blasphemies with which they may blaspheme; ²⁹but whoever may blaspheme against the Holy Spirit never has forgiveness, but is subject to eternal condemnation." ³⁰—because they said, "He has an unclean spirit."

3:31 H<small>IS</small> mother and his brothers came, and standing outside, they sent to him, calling him. [32]A multitude was sitting around him, and they told him, "Behold, your mother, your brothers, and your sisters are outside looking for you."

[33]He answered them, "Who are my mother and my brothers?" [34]Looking around at those who sat around him, he said, "Behold, my mother and my brothers! [35]For whoever does the will of God is my brother, my sister, and mother."

CHAPTER FOUR

[1]Again he began to teach by the seaside. A great multitude was gathered to him, so that he entered into a boat in the sea, and sat down. All the multitude were on the land by the sea.

4:2 HE taught them many things in parables, and told them in his teaching, ³ "Listen! Behold, the farmer went out to sow, ⁴and as he sowed, some seed fell by the road, and the birds came and devoured it. ⁵Others fell on the rocky ground, where it had little soil, and immediately it sprang up, because it had no depth of soil. ⁶When the sun had risen, it was scorched; and because it had no root, it withered away. ⁷Others fell among the thorns, and the thorns grew up, and choked it, and it yielded no fruit. ⁸Others fell into the good ground, and yielded fruit, growing up and increasing. Some produced thirty times, some sixty times, and some one hundred times as much." ⁹He said, "Whoever has ears to hear, let him hear."

4:10 WHEN he was alone, those who were around him with the twelve asked him about the parables. [11]He said to them, "To you is given the mystery of God's Kingdom, but to those who are outside, all things are done in parables, [12]that 'seeing they may see, and not perceive; and hearing they may hear, and not understand; lest perhaps they should turn again, and their sins should be forgiven them.'"

[13]He said to them, "Don't you understand this parable? How will you understand all of the parables? [14]The farmer sows the word. [15]The ones by the road are the ones where the word is sown; and when they have heard, immediately Satan comes, and takes away the word which has been sown in them. [16]These in the same way are those who are sown on the rocky places, who, when they have heard the word, immediately receive it with joy. [17]They have no root in themselves, but are short-lived. When oppression or persecution arises because of the word, immediately they stumble. [18]Others are those who are sown among the thorns. These are those who have heard the word, [19]and the cares of this age, and the deceitfulness of riches, and the lusts of other things entering in choke the word, and it becomes unfruitful. [20]Those which were sown on the good ground are those who hear the word, and accept it, and bear fruit, some thirty times, some sixty times, and some one hundred times."

4:21 HE said to them, "Is the lamp brought to be put under a basket or under a bed? Isn't it put on a stand? ²²For there is nothing hidden, except that it should be made known; neither was anything made secret, but that it should come to light. ²³If any man has ears to hear, let him hear."

4:24 HE said to them, "Take heed what you hear. With whatever measure you measure, it will be measured to you, and more will be given to you who hear. ²⁵For whoever has, to him more will be given, and he who doesn't have, even that which he has will be taken away from him."

4:26 HE SAID, "God's Kingdom is as if a man should cast seed on the earth, ²⁷and should sleep and rise night and day, and the seed should spring up and grow, though he doesn't know how. ²⁸For the earth bears fruit: first the blade, then the ear, then the full grain in the ear. ²⁹But when the fruit is ripe, immediately he puts in the sickle, because the harvest has come."

4:30 HE SAID, "How will we liken God's Kingdom? Or with what parable will we illustrate it? ³¹It's like a grain of mustard seed, which, when it is sown in the earth, though it is less than all the seeds that are on the earth, ³²yet when it is sown, grows up, and becomes greater than all the herbs, and puts out great branches, so that the birds of the sky can lodge under its shadow."

4:33 With many such parables he spoke the word to them, as they were able to hear it. ³⁴Without a parable he didn't speak to them; but privately to his own disciples he explained everything.

4:35 ON THAT DAY, when evening had come, he said to them, "Let's go over to the other side." ³⁶Leaving the multitude, they took him with them, even as he was, in the boat. Other small boats were also with him. ³⁷A big wind storm arose, and the waves beat into the boat, so much that the boat was already filled. ³⁸He himself was in the stern, asleep on the cushion, and they woke him up, and told him, "Teacher, don't you care that we are dying?"

³⁹He awoke, and rebuked the wind, and said to the sea, "Peace! Be still!" The wind ceased, and there was a great calm. ⁴⁰He said to them, "Why are you so afraid? How is it that you have no faith?"

⁴¹They were greatly afraid, and said to one another, "Who then is this, that even the wind and the sea obey him?"

CHAPTER FIVE

¹They came to the other side of the sea, into the country of the Gadarenes. ²When he had come out of the boat, immediately a man with an unclean spirit met him out of the tombs. ³He lived in the tombs. Nobody could bind him any more, not even with chains, ⁴because he had been often bound with fetters and chains, and the chains had been torn apart by him, and the fetters broken in pieces. Nobody had the strength to tame him. ⁵Always, night and day, in the tombs and in the mountains, he was crying out, and cutting himself with stones. ⁶When he saw Jesus from afar, he ran and bowed down to him, ⁷and crying out with a loud voice, he said, "What have I to do with you, Jesus, you Son of the Most High God? I adjure you by God, don't torment me." ⁸For he said to him, "Come out of the man, you unclean spirit!"

⁹He asked him, "What is your name?"

He said to him, "My name is Legion, for we are many." ¹⁰He begged him much that he would not send them away out of the country. ¹¹Now on the mountainside there was a great herd of pigs feeding. ¹²All the demons begged him, saying, "Send us into the pigs, that we may enter into them."

¹³At once Jesus gave them permission. The unclean spirits came out and entered into the pigs. The herd of about two thousand rushed down the steep bank into the sea, and they were drowned in the sea.

5:14 Those who fed them fled, and told it in the city and in the country.

The people came to see what it was that had happened. ¹⁵They came to Jesus, and saw him who had been possessed by demons sitting, clothed, and in his right mind, even him who had the legion; and they were afraid. ¹⁶Those who saw it declared to them what happened to him who was possessed by demons, and about the pigs. ¹⁷They began to beg him to depart from their region.

¹⁸As he was entering into the boat, he who had been possessed by demons begged him that he might be with him. ¹⁹He didn't allow him, but said to him, "Go to your house, to your friends, and tell them what great things the Lord has done for you, and how he had mercy on you."

²⁰He went his way, and began to proclaim in Decapolis how Jesus had done great things for him, and everyone marveled.

5:21 When Jesus had crossed back over in the boat to the other side, a great multitude was gathered to him; and he was by the sea. ²²Behold, one of the rulers of the synagogue, Jairus by name, came; and seeing him, he fell at his feet, ²³and begged him much, saying, "My little daughter is at the point of death. Please come and lay your hands on her, that she may be made healthy, and live."

²⁴He went with him, and a great multitude followed him, and they pressed upon him on all sides. ²⁵A certain woman, who had a discharge of blood for twelve years, ²⁶and had suffered many things by many physicians, and had spent all that she had, and was no better, but rather grew worse, ²⁷having heard the things concerning Jesus, came up behind him in the crowd, and touched his clothes. ²⁸For she said, "If I just touch his clothes, I will be made well." ²⁹Immediately the flow of her blood was dried up, and she felt in her body that she was healed of her affliction.

³⁰Immediately Jesus, perceiving in himself that the power had gone out from him, turned around in the crowd, and asked, "Who touched my clothes?"

³¹His disciples said to him, "You see the multitude pressing against you, and you say, 'Who touched me?'"

³²He looked around to see her who had done this thing. ³³But the woman, fearing and trembling, knowing what had been done to her, came and fell down before him, and told him all the truth.

³⁴He said to her, "Daughter, your faith has made you well. Go in peace, and be cured of your disease."

5:35 WHILE he was still speaking, people came from the synagogue ruler's house saying, "Your daughter is dead. Why bother the Teacher any more?"

³⁶But Jesus, when he heard the message spoken, immediately said to the ruler of the synagogue, "Don't be afraid, only believe." ³⁷He allowed no one to follow him, except Peter, James, and John the brother of James. ³⁸He came to the synagogue ruler's house, and he saw an uproar, weeping, and great wailing. ³⁹When he had entered in, he said to them, "Why do you make an uproar and weep? The child is not dead, but is asleep."

⁴⁰They ridiculed him. But he, having put them all out, took the father of the child, her mother, and those who were with him, and went in where the child was lying. ⁴¹Taking the child by the hand, he said to her, "Talitha cumi!" which means, being interpreted, "Girl, I tell you, get up!" ⁴²Immediately the girl rose up and walked, for she was twelve years old. They were amazed with great amazement. ⁴³He strictly ordered them that no one should know this, and commanded that something should be given to her to eat.

CHAPTER SIX

¹He went out from there. He came into his own country, and his disciples followed him. ²When the Sabbath had come, he began to teach in the synagogue, and many hearing him were astonished, saying, "Where did this man get these things?" and, "What is the wisdom that is given to this man, that such mighty works come about by his hands? ³Isn't this the carpenter, the son of Mary, and brother of James, Joses, Judah, and Simon? Aren't his sisters here with us?" They were offended at him.

⁴Jesus said to them, "A prophet is not without honor, except in his own country, and among his own relatives, and in his own house." ⁵He could do no mighty work there, except that he laid his hands on a few sick people, and healed them. ⁶He marveled because of their unbelief.

He went around the villages teaching.

6:7 HE CALLED to himself the twelve, and began to send them out two by two; and he gave them authority over the unclean spirits. ⁸He commanded them that they should take nothing for their journey, except a staff only: no bread, no wallet, no money in their purse, ⁹but to wear sandals, and not put on two tunics. ¹⁰He said to them, "Wherever you enter into a house, stay there until you depart from there. ¹¹Whoever will not receive you nor hear you, as you depart from there, shake off the dust that is under your feet for a testimony against them. Assuredly, I tell you, it will be more tolerable for Sodom and Gomorrah in the day of judgment than for that city!"

¹²They went out and preached that people should repent. ¹³They cast out many demons, and anointed many with oil who were sick, and healed them.

6:14 KING Herod heard this, for his name had become known, and he said, "John the Baptizer has risen from the dead, and therefore these powers are at work in him." ¹⁵But others said, "He is Elijah." Others said, "He is a prophet, or like one of the prophets." ¹⁶But Herod, when he heard this, said, "This is John, whom I beheaded. He has risen from the dead."

¹⁷For Herod himself had sent out and arrested John, and bound him in prison for the sake of Herodias, his brother Philip's wife, for he had married her. ¹⁸For John said to Herod, "It is not lawful for you to have your brother's wife." ¹⁹Herodias set herself against him, and desired to kill him, but she couldn't, ²⁰for Herod feared John, knowing that he was a righteous and holy man, and kept him safe. When he heard him, he did many things, and he heard him gladly.

6:21 THEN A CONVENIENT day came, that Herod on his birthday made a supper for his nobles, the high officers, and the chief men of Galilee. ²²When the daughter of Herodias herself came in and danced, she pleased Herod and those sitting with him. The king said to the young lady, "Ask me whatever you want, and I will give it to you." ²³He swore to her, "Whatever you shall ask of me, I will give you, up to half of my kingdom."

²⁴She went out, and said to her mother, "What shall I ask?"

She said, "The head of John the Baptizer."

²⁵She came in immediately with haste to the king, and asked, "I want you to give me right now the head of John the Baptizer on a platter."

²⁶The king was exceedingly sorry, but for the sake of his oaths, and of his dinner guests, he didn't wish to refuse her. ²⁷Immediately the king sent out a soldier of his guard, and commanded to bring John's head, and he went and beheaded him in the prison, ²⁸and brought his head on a platter, and gave it to the young lady; and the young lady gave it to her mother.

²⁹When his disciples heard this, they came and took up his corpse, and laid it in a tomb.

6:30 THE apostles gathered themselves together to Jesus, and they told him all things, whatever they had done, and whatever they had taught. ³¹He said to them, "You come apart into a deserted place, and rest awhile." For there were many coming and going, and they had no leisure so much as to eat. ³²They went away in the boat to a deserted place by themselves.

³³They saw them going, and many recognized him and ran there on foot from all the cities. They arrived before them and came together to him. ³⁴Jesus came out, saw a great multitude, and he had compassion on them, because they were like sheep without a shepherd, and he began to teach them many things.

6:35 WHEN it was late in the day, his disciples came to him, and said, "This place is deserted, and it is late in the day. ³⁶Send them away, that they may go into the surrounding country and villages, and buy themselves bread, for they have nothing to eat."

³⁷But he answered them, "You give them something to eat."

They asked him, "Shall we go and buy two hundred denarii worth of bread, and give them something to eat?"

³⁸He said to them, "How many loaves do you have? Go see."

When they knew, they said, "Five, and two fish."

³⁹He commanded them that everyone should sit down in groups on the green grass. ⁴⁰They sat down in ranks, by hundreds and by fifties. ⁴¹He took the five loaves and the two fish, and looking up to heaven, he blessed and broke the loaves, and he gave to his disciples to set before them, and he divided the two fish among them all. ⁴²They all ate, and were filled. ⁴³They took up twelve baskets full of broken pieces and also of the fish. ⁴⁴Those who ate the loaves were five thousand men.

6:45 IMMEDIATELY HE made his disciples get into the boat, and to go ahead to the other side, to Bethsaida, while he himself sent the multitude away. [46]After he had taken leave of them, he went up the mountain to pray.

[47]When evening had come, the boat was in the middle of the sea, and he was alone on the land. [48]Seeing them distressed in rowing, for the wind was contrary to them, about the fourth watch of the night he came to them, walking on the sea, and he would have passed by them, [49]but they, when they saw him walking on the sea, supposed that it was a ghost, and cried out; [50]for they all saw him, and were troubled. But he immediately spoke with them, and said to them, "Cheer up! It is I! Don't be afraid." [51]He got into the boat with them; and the wind ceased, and they were very amazed among themselves, and marveled; [52]for they hadn't understood about the loaves, but their hearts were hardened.

6:53 WHEN they had crossed over, they came to land at Gennesaret, and moored to the shore. [54]When they had come out of the boat, immediately the people recognized him, [55]and ran around that whole region, and began to bring those who were sick, on their mats, to where they heard he was. [56]Wherever he entered, into villages, or into cities, or into the country, they laid the sick in the marketplaces, and begged him that they might just touch the fringe of his garment; and as many as touched him were made well.

CHAPTER SEVEN

¹Then the Pharisees and some of the scribes gathered together to him, having come from Jerusalem. ²Now when they saw some of his disciples eating bread with defiled, that is unwashed, hands, they found fault. ³(For the Pharisees and all the Jews don't eat unless they wash their hands and forearms, holding to the tradition of the elders. ⁴They don't eat when they come from the marketplace unless they bathe themselves, and there are many other things, which they have received to hold to: washings of cups, pitchers, bronze vessels, and couches.)

⁵The Pharisees and the scribes asked him, "Why don't your disciples walk according to the tradition of the elders, but eat their bread with unwashed hands?"

⁶He answered them, "Well did Isaiah prophesy of you hypocrites, as it is written,

'This people honors me with their lips,
but their heart is far from me.
⁷But they worship me in vain,
teaching as doctrines the commandments of men.'

⁸"For you set aside the commandment of God, and hold tightly to the tradition of men—the washing of pitchers and cups, and you do many other such things."

7:9 He said to them, "Full well do you reject the commandment of God, that you may keep your tradition. ¹⁰For Moses said, 'Honor your father and your mother;' and, 'He who speaks evil of father or mother, let him be put to death.' ¹¹But you say, 'If a man tells his father or his mother, "Whatever profit you might have received from me is Corban,"'" that is to say, given to God, ¹²"then you no longer allow him to do anything for his father or his mother, ¹³making void the word of God by your tradition, which you have handed down. You do many things like this."

7:14 He called all the multitude to himself, and said to them, "Hear me, all of you, and understand. ¹⁵There is nothing from outside of the man, that going into him can defile him; but the things which proceed out of the man are those that defile the man. ¹⁶If anyone has ears to hear, let him hear!"

7:17 WHEN he had entered into a house away from the multitude, his disciples asked him about the parable. [18]He said to them, "Are you also without understanding? Don't you perceive that whatever goes into the man from outside can't defile him, [19]because it doesn't go into his heart, but into his stomach, then into the latrine, making all foods clean?" [20]He said, "That which proceeds out of the man, that defiles the man. [21]For from within, out of the hearts of men, proceed evil thoughts, adulteries, sexual sins, murders, thefts, [22]covetings, wickedness, deceit, lustful desires, an evil eye, blasphemy, pride, and foolishness. [23]All these evil things come from within, and defile the man."

7:24 F<small>ROM</small> there he arose, and went away into the borders of Tyre and Sidon. He entered into a house, and didn't want anyone to know it, but he couldn't escape notice. ²⁵For a woman, whose little daughter had an unclean spirit, having heard of him, came and fell down at his feet. ²⁶Now the woman was a Greek, a Syrophoenician by race. She begged him that he would cast the demon out of her daughter. ²⁷But Jesus said to her, "Let the children be filled first, for it is not appropriate to take the children's bread and throw it to the dogs."

²⁸But she answered him, "Yes, Lord. Yet even the dogs under the table eat the children's crumbs."

²⁹He said to her, "For this saying, go your way. The demon has gone out of your daughter."

³⁰She went away to her house, and found the child having been laid on the bed, with the demon gone out.

7:31 AGAIN he departed from the borders of Tyre and Sidon, and came to the sea of Galilee, through the middle of the region of Decapolis. ³²They brought to him one who was deaf and had an impediment in his speech. They begged him to lay his hand on him. ³³He took him aside from the multitude, privately, and put his fingers into his ears, and he spat, and touched his tongue. ³⁴Looking up to heaven, he sighed, and said to him, "Ephphatha!" that is, "Be opened!" ³⁵Immediately his ears were opened, and the impediment of his tongue was released, and he spoke clearly. ³⁶He commanded them that they should tell no one, but the more he commanded them, so much the more widely they proclaimed it. ³⁷They were astonished beyond measure, saying, "He has done all things well. He makes even the deaf hear, and the mute speak!"

CHAPTER EIGHT

¹In those days, when there was a very great multitude, and they had nothing to eat, Jesus called his disciples to himself, and said to them, ²"I have compassion on the multitude, because they have stayed with me now three days, and have nothing to eat. ³If I send them away fasting to their home, they will faint on the way, for some of them have come a long way."

⁴His disciples answered him, "From where could one satisfy these people with bread here in a deserted place?"

⁵He asked them, "How many loaves do you have?"

They said, "Seven."

⁶He commanded the multitude to sit down on the ground, and he took the seven loaves. Having given thanks, he broke them, and gave them to his disciples to serve, and they served the multitude. ⁷They had a few small fish. Having blessed them, he said to serve these also. ⁸They ate, and were filled. They took up seven baskets of broken pieces that were left over. ⁹Those who had eaten were about four thousand. Then he sent them away.

8:10 IMMEDIATELY HE entered into the boat with his disciples, and came into the region of Dalmanutha. [11]The Pharisees came out and began to question him, seeking from him a sign from heaven, and testing him. [12]He sighed deeply in his spirit, and said, "Why does this generation seek a sign? Most certainly I tell you, no sign will be given to this generation."

8:13 He left them, and again entering into the boat, departed to the other side. ¹⁴They forgot to take bread; and they didn't have more than one loaf in the boat with them. ¹⁵He warned them, saying, "Take heed: beware of the yeast of the Pharisees and the yeast of Herod."

¹⁶They reasoned with one another, saying, "It's because we have no bread."

¹⁷Jesus, perceiving it, said to them, "Why do you reason that it's because you have no bread? Don't you perceive yet, neither understand? Is your heart still hardened? ¹⁸Having eyes, don't you see? Having ears, don't you hear? Don't you remember? ¹⁹When I broke the five loaves among the five thousand, how many baskets full of broken pieces did you take up?"

They told him, "Twelve."

²⁰"When the seven loaves fed the four thousand, how many baskets full of broken pieces did you take up?"

They told him, "Seven."

²¹He asked them, "Don't you understand yet?"

8:22 H<small>E</small> came to Bethsaida. They brought a blind man to him, and begged him to touch him. ²³He took hold of the blind man by the hand, and brought him out of the village. When he had spat on his eyes, and laid his hands on him, he asked him if he saw anything.

²⁴He looked up, and said, "I see men; for I see them like trees walking."

²⁵Then again he laid his hands on his eyes. He looked intently, and was restored, and saw everyone clearly. ²⁶He sent him away to his house, saying, "Don't enter into the village, nor tell anyone in the village."

8:27 JESUS WENT OUT, with his disciples, into the villages of Caesarea Philippi. On the way he asked his disciples, "Who do men say that I am?"

[28]They told him, "John the Baptizer, and others say Elijah, but others: one of the prophets."

[29]He said to them, "But who do you say that I am?"

Peter answered, "You are the Christ."

[30]He commanded them that they should tell no one about him. [31]He began to teach them that the Son of Man must suffer many things, and be rejected by the elders, the chief priests, and the scribes, and be killed, and after three days rise again. [32]He spoke to them openly. Peter took him, and began to rebuke him. [33]But he, turning around, and seeing his disciples, rebuked Peter, and said, "Get behind me, Satan! For you have in mind not the things of God, but the things of men."

8:34 He called the multitude to himself with his disciples, and said to them, "Whoever wants to come after me, let him deny himself, and take up his cross, and follow me. ³⁵For whoever wants to save his life will lose it; and whoever will lose his life for my sake and the sake of the Good News will save it. ³⁶For what does it profit a man, to gain the whole world, and forfeit his life? ³⁷For what will a man give in exchange for his life? ³⁸For whoever will be ashamed of me and of my words in this adulterous and sinful generation, the Son of Man also will be ashamed of him, when he comes in his Father's glory, with the holy angels."

Chapter Nine

¹He said to them, "Most certainly I tell you, there are some standing here who will in no way taste death until they see God's Kingdom come with power."

9:2 AFTER SIX days Jesus took with him Peter, James, and John, and brought them up onto a high mountain privately by themselves, and he was changed into another form in front of them. ³His clothing became glistening, exceedingly white, like snow, such as no launderer on earth can whiten them. ⁴Elijah and Moses appeared to them, and they were talking with Jesus.

⁵Peter answered Jesus, "Rabbi, it is good for us to be here. Let's make three tents: one for you, one for Moses, and one for Elijah." ⁶For he didn't know what to say, for they were very afraid.

⁷A cloud came, overshadowing them, and a voice came out of the cloud, "This is my beloved Son. Listen to him."

⁸Suddenly looking around, they saw no one with them any more, except Jesus only.

9:9 As THEY were coming down from the mountain, he commanded them that they should tell no one what things they had seen, until after the Son of Man had risen from the dead. ¹⁰They kept this saying to themselves, questioning what the "rising from the dead" meant.

¹¹They asked him, saying, "Why do the scribes say that Elijah must come first?"

¹²He said to them, "Elijah indeed comes first, and restores all things. How is it written about the Son of Man, that he should suffer many things and be despised? ¹³But I tell you that Elijah has come, and they have also done to him whatever they wanted to, even as it is written about him."

¹⁴Coming to the disciples, he saw a great multitude around them, and scribes questioning them. ¹⁵Immediately all the multitude, when they saw him, were greatly amazed, and running to him, greeted him. ¹⁶He asked the scribes, "What are you asking them?"

9:17 ONE of the multitude answered, "Teacher, I brought to you my son, who has a mute spirit; [18]and wherever it seizes him, it throws him down, and he foams at the mouth, and grinds his teeth, and wastes away. I asked your disciples to cast it out, and they weren't able."

[19]He answered him, "Unbelieving generation, how long shall I be with you? How long shall I bear with you? Bring him to me."

[20]They brought him to him, and when he saw him, immediately the spirit convulsed him, and he fell on the ground, wallowing and foaming at the mouth.

[21]He asked his father, "How long has it been since this has come to him?"

He said, "From childhood. [22]Often it has cast him both into the fire and into the water to destroy him. But if you can do anything, have compassion on us, and help us."

[23]Jesus said to him, "If you can believe, all things are possible to him who believes."

[24]Immediately the father of the child cried out with tears, "I believe. Help my unbelief!"

[25]When Jesus saw that a multitude came running together, he rebuked the unclean spirit, saying to him, "You mute and deaf spirit, I command you, come out of him, and never enter him again!"

[26]After crying out and convulsing him greatly, it came out of him. The boy became like one dead, so much that most of them said, "He is dead." [27]But Jesus took him by the hand, and raised him up; and he arose.

9:28 WHEN he had come into the house, his disciples asked him privately, "Why couldn't we cast it out?" ²⁹He said to them, "This kind can come out by nothing, except by prayer and fasting."

9:30 THEY went out from there, and passed through Galilee. He didn't want anyone to know it. [31]For he was teaching his disciples, and said to them, "The Son of Man is being handed over to the hands of men, and they will kill him; and when he is killed, on the third day he will rise again."

[32]But they didn't understand the saying, and were afraid to ask him.

9:33 HE came to Capernaum, and when he was in the house he asked them, "What were you arguing among yourselves on the way?"

³⁴But they were silent, for they had disputed with one another on the way about who was the greatest.

³⁵He sat down, and called the twelve; and he said to them, "If any man wants to be first, he shall be last of all, and servant of all." ³⁶He took a little child, and set him in the middle of them. Taking him in his arms, he said to them, ³⁷"Whoever receives one such little child in my name, receives me, and whoever receives me, doesn't receive me, but him who sent me."

9:38 JOHN said to him, "Teacher, we saw someone who doesn't follow us casting out demons in your name; and we forbade him, because he doesn't follow us."

³⁹But Jesus said, "Don't forbid him, for there is no one who will do a mighty work in my name, and be able quickly to speak evil of me. ⁴⁰For whoever is not against us is on our side. ⁴¹For whoever will give you a cup of water to drink in my name, because you are Christ's, most certainly I tell you, he will in no way lose his reward.

9:42 WHOEVER will cause one of these little ones who believe in me to stumble, it would be better for him if he were thrown into the sea with a millstone hung around his neck.

⁴³If your hand causes you to stumble, cut it off. It is better for you to enter into life maimed, rather than having your two hands to go into Gehenna, into the unquenchable fire, ⁴⁴'where their worm doesn't die, and the fire is not quenched.'

⁴⁵If your foot causes you to stumble, cut it off. It is better for you to enter into life lame, rather than having your two feet to be cast into Gehenna, into the fire that will never be quenched— ⁴⁶'where their worm doesn't die, and the fire is not quenched.'

⁴⁷If your eye causes you to stumble, cast it out. It is better for you to enter into God's Kingdom with one eye, rather than having two eyes to be cast into the Gehenna of fire, ⁴⁸'where their worm doesn't die, and the fire is not quenched.'

⁴⁹For everyone will be salted with fire, and every sacrifice will be seasoned with salt. ⁵⁰Salt is good, but if the salt has lost its saltiness, with what will you season it? Have salt in yourselves, and be at peace with one another."

CHAPTER TEN

¹He arose from there and came into the borders of Judea and beyond the Jordan. Multitudes came together to him again. As he usually did, he was again teaching them. ²Pharisees came to him testing him, and asked him, "Is it lawful for a man to divorce his wife?"

³He answered, "What did Moses command you?"

⁴They said, "Moses allowed a certificate of divorce to be written, and to divorce her."

⁵But Jesus said to them, "For your hardness of heart, he wrote you this commandment. ⁶But from the beginning of the creation, God made them male and female. ⁷For this cause a man will leave his father and mother, and will join to his wife, ⁸and the two will become one flesh, so that they are no longer two, but one flesh. ⁹What therefore God has joined together, let no man separate."

10:10 IN THE HOUSE, his disciples asked him again about the same matter. [11]He said to them, "Whoever divorces his wife, and marries another, commits adultery against her. [12]If a woman herself divorces her husband, and marries another, she commits adultery."

10:13 THEY were bringing to him little children, that he should touch them, but the disciples rebuked those who were bringing them. ¹⁴But when Jesus saw it, he was moved with indignation, and said to them, "Allow the little children to come to me! Don't forbid them, for God's Kingdom belongs to such as these. ¹⁵Most certainly I tell you, whoever will not receive God's Kingdom like a little child, he will in no way enter into it." ¹⁶He took them in his arms, and blessed them, laying his hands on them.

10:17 As he was going out into the way, one ran to him, knelt before him, and asked him, "Good Teacher, what shall I do that I may inherit eternal life?"

[18]Jesus said to him, "Why do you call me good? No one is good except one—God. [19]You know the commandments: 'Do not murder,' 'Do not commit adultery,' 'Do not steal,' 'Do not give false testimony,' 'Do not defraud,' 'Honor your father and mother.'"

[20]He said to him, "Teacher, I have observed all these things from my youth."

[21]Jesus looking at him loved him, and said to him, "One thing you lack. Go, sell whatever you have, and give to the poor, and you will have treasure in heaven; and come, follow me, taking up the cross."

[22]But his face fell at that saying, and he went away sorrowful, for he was one who had great possessions. [23]Jesus looked around, and said to his disciples, "How difficult it is for those who have riches to enter into God's Kingdom!"

10:24 THE disciples were amazed at his words. But Jesus answered again, "Children, how hard it is for those who trust in riches to enter into God's Kingdom! [25]It is easier for a camel to go through a needle's eye than for a rich man to enter into God's Kingdom."

[26]They were exceedingly astonished, saying to him, "Then who can be saved?"

[27]Jesus, looking at them, said, "With men it is impossible, but not with God, for all things are possible with God."

[28]Peter began to tell him, "Behold, we have left all, and have followed you."

[29]Jesus said, "Most certainly I tell you, there is no one who has left house, or brothers, or sisters, or father, or mother, or wife, or children, or land, for my sake, and for the sake of the Good News, [30]but he will receive one hundred times more now in this time: houses, brothers, sisters, mothers, children, and land, with persecutions; and in the age to come eternal life. [31]But many who are first will be last; and the last first."

10:32 THEY were on the way, going up to Jerusalem; and Jesus was going in front of them, and they were amazed; and those who followed were afraid. He again took the twelve, and began to tell them the things that were going to happen to him. ³³"Behold, we are going up to Jerusalem. The Son of Man will be delivered to the chief priests and the scribes. They will condemn him to death, and will deliver him to the Gentiles. ³⁴They will mock him, spit on him, scourge him, and kill him. On the third day he will rise again."

10:35 JAMES AND JOHN, the sons of Zebedee, came near to him, saying, "Teacher, we want you to do for us whatever we will ask."

³⁶He said to them, "What do you want me to do for you?"

³⁷They said to him, "Grant to us that we may sit, one at your right hand, and one at your left hand, in your glory."

³⁸But Jesus said to them, "You don't know what you are asking. Are you able to drink the cup that I drink, and to be baptized with the baptism that I am baptized with?"

³⁹They said to him, "We are able."

Jesus said to them, "You shall indeed drink the cup that I drink, and you shall be baptized with the baptism that I am baptized with; ⁴⁰but to sit at my right hand and at my left hand is not mine to give, but for whom it has been prepared."

10:41 When the ten heard it, they began to be indignant toward James and John.

⁴²Jesus summoned them, and said to them, "You know that they who are recognized as rulers over the nations lord it over them, and their great ones exercise authority over them. ⁴³But it shall not be so among you, but whoever wants to become great among you shall be your servant. ⁴⁴Whoever of you wants to become first among you, shall be bondservant of all. ⁴⁵For the Son of Man also came not to be served, but to serve, and to give his life as a ransom for many."

10:46 THEY came to Jericho. As he went out from Jericho, with his disciples and a great multitude, the son of Timaeus, Bartimaeus, a blind beggar, was sitting by the road. ⁴⁷When he heard that it was Jesus the Nazarene, he began to cry out, and say, "Jesus, you son of David, have mercy on me!" ⁴⁸Many rebuked him, that he should be quiet, but he cried out much more, "You son of David, have mercy on me!"

⁴⁹Jesus stood still, and said, "Call him."

They called the blind man, saying to him, "Cheer up! Get up. He is calling you!"

⁵⁰He, casting away his cloak, sprang up, and came to Jesus.

⁵¹Jesus asked him, "What do you want me to do for you?"

The blind man said to him, "Rabboni, that I may see again."

⁵²Jesus said to him, "Go your way. Your faith has made you well." Immediately he received his sight, and followed Jesus on the way.

CHAPTER ELEVEN

¹When they came near to Jerusalem, to Bethsphage and Bethany, at the Mount of Olives, he sent two of his disciples, ²and said to them, "Go your way into the village that is opposite you. Immediately as you enter into it, you will find a young donkey tied, on which no one has sat. Untie him, and bring him. ³If anyone asks you, 'Why are you doing this?' say, 'The Lord needs him;' and immediately he will send him back here."

⁴They went away, and found a young donkey tied at the door outside in the open street, and they untied him. ⁵Some of those who stood there asked them, "What are you doing, untying the young donkey?" ⁶They said to them just as Jesus had said, and they let them go.

11:7 THEY BROUGHT the young donkey to Jesus, and threw their garments on it, and Jesus sat on it. ⁸Many spread their garments on the way, and others were cutting down branches from the trees, and spreading them on the road. ⁹Those who went in front, and those who followed, cried out, "Hosanna! Blessed is he who comes in the name of the Lord! ¹⁰Blessed is the kingdom of our father David that is coming in the name of the Lord! Hosanna in the highest!"

¹¹Jesus entered into the temple in Jerusalem. When he had looked around at everything, it being now evening, he went out to Bethany with the twelve.

11:12 THE NEXT DAY, when they had come out from Bethany, he was hungry. ¹³Seeing a fig tree afar off having leaves, he came to see if perhaps he might find anything on it. When he came to it, he found nothing but leaves, for it was not the season for figs. ¹⁴Jesus told it, "May no one ever eat fruit from you again!" and his disciples heard it.

¹⁵They came to Jerusalem, and Jesus entered into the temple, and began to throw out those who sold and those who bought in the temple, and overthrew the money changers' tables, and the seats of those who sold the doves. ¹⁶He would not allow anyone to carry a container through the temple. ¹⁷He taught, saying to them, "Isn't it written, 'My house will be called a house of prayer for all the nations?' But you have made it a den of robbers!"

¹⁸The chief priests and the scribes heard it, and sought how they might destroy him. For they feared him, because all the multitude was astonished at his teaching.

¹⁹ When evening came, he went out of the city.

11:20 As they passed by in the morning, they saw the fig tree withered away from the roots. [21]Peter, remembering, said to him, "Rabbi, look! The fig tree which you cursed has withered away."

[22]Jesus answered them, "Have faith in God. [23]For most certainly I tell you, whoever may tell this mountain, 'Be taken up and cast into the sea,' and doesn't doubt in his heart, but believes that what he says is happening; he shall have whatever he says. [24]Therefore I tell you, all things whatever you pray and ask for, believe that you have received them, and you shall have them. [25]Whenever you stand praying, forgive, if you have anything against anyone; so that your Father, who is in heaven, may also forgive you your transgressions. [26]But if you do not forgive, neither will your Father in heaven forgive your transgressions."

11:27 THEY came again to Jerusalem, and as he was walking in the temple, the chief priests, the scribes, and the elders came to him, ²⁸and they began saying to him, "By what authority do you do these things? Or who gave you this authority to do these things?"

²⁹Jesus said to them, "I will ask you one question. Answer me, and I will tell you by what authority I do these things. ³⁰The baptism of John—was it from heaven, or from men? Answer me."

³¹They reasoned with themselves, saying, "If we should say, 'From heaven;' he will say, 'Why then did you not believe him?' ³²If we should say, 'From men'"—they feared the people, for all held John to really be a prophet. ³³They answered Jesus, "We don't know."

Jesus said to them, "Neither do I tell you by what authority I do these things."

CHAPTER TWELVE

¹He began to speak to them in parables. "A man planted a vineyard, put a hedge around it, dug a pit for the wine press, built a tower, rented it out to a farmer, and went into another country. ²When it was time, he sent a servant to the farmer to get from the farmer his share of the fruit of the vineyard. ³They took him, beat him, and sent him away empty. ⁴Again, he sent another servant to them; and they threw stones at him, wounded him in the head, and sent him away shamefully treated. ⁵Again he sent another; and they killed him; and many others, beating some, and killing some. ⁶Therefore still having one, his beloved son, he sent him last to them, saying, 'They will respect my son.' ⁷But those farmers said among themselves, 'This is the heir. Come, let's kill him, and the inheritance will be ours.' ⁸They took him, killed him, and cast him out of the vineyard. ⁹What therefore will the lord of the vineyard do? He will come and destroy the farmers, and will give the vineyard to others. ¹⁰Haven't you even read this Scripture:

'The stone which the builders rejected
was made the head of the corner.
¹¹This was from the Lord.
It is marvelous in our eyes'?"

¹²They tried to seize him, but they feared the multitude; for they perceived that he spoke the parable against them. They left him, and went away.

12:13 THEY sent some of the Pharisees and the Herodians to him, that they might trap him with words. ¹⁴When they had come, they asked him, "Teacher, we know that you are honest, and don't defer to anyone; for you aren't partial to anyone, but truly teach the way of God. Is it lawful to pay taxes to Caesar, or not? ¹⁵Shall we give, or shall we not give?"

But he, knowing their hypocrisy, said to them, "Why do you test me? Bring me a denarius, that I may see it."

¹⁶They brought it.

He said to them, "Whose is this image and inscription?"

They said to him, "Caesar's."

¹⁷Jesus answered them, "Render to Caesar the things that are Caesar's, and to God the things that are God's."

They marveled greatly at him.

12:18 SOME SADDUCEES, who say that there is no resurrection, came to him. They asked him, saying, [19]"Teacher, Moses wrote to us, 'If a man's brother dies, and leaves a wife behind him, and leaves no children, that his brother should take his wife, and raise up offspring for his brother.' [20]There were seven brothers. The first took a wife, and dying left no offspring. [21]The second took her, and died, leaving no children behind him. The third likewise; [22]and the seven took her and left no children. Last of all the woman also died. [23]In the resurrection, when they rise, whose wife will she be of them? For the seven had her as a wife."

[24]Jesus answered them, "Isn't this because you are mistaken, not knowing the Scriptures, nor the power of God? [25]For when they will rise from the dead, they neither marry, nor are given in marriage, but are like angels in heaven. [26]But about the dead, that they are raised; haven't you read in the book of Moses, about the Bush, how God spoke to him, saying, 'I am the God of Abraham, the God of Isaac, and the God of Jacob'? [27]He is not the God of the dead, but of the living. You are therefore badly mistaken."

12:28 ONE of the scribes came, and heard them questioning together, and knowing that he had answered them well, asked him, "Which commandment is the greatest of all?"

²⁹Jesus answered, "The greatest is, 'Hear, Israel, the Lord our God, the Lord is one: ³⁰you shall love the Lord your God with all your heart, and with all your soul, and with all your mind, and with all your strength.' This is the first commandment. ³¹The second is like this, 'You shall love your neighbor as yourself.' There is no other commandment greater than these."

³²The scribe said to him, "Truly, teacher, you have said well that he is one, and there is none other but he, ³³and to love him with all the heart, and with all the understanding, with all the soul, and with all the strength, and to love his neighbor as himself, is more important than all whole burnt offerings and sacrifices."

³⁴When Jesus saw that he answered wisely, he said to him, "You are not far from God's Kingdom."

No one dared ask him any question after that.

12:35 Jesus responded, as he taught in the temple, "How is it that the scribes say that the Christ is the son of David? ³⁶For David himself said in the Holy Spirit,

'The Lord said to my Lord,

"Sit at my right hand,

until I make your enemies the footstool of your feet."'

³⁷Therefore David himself calls him Lord, so how can he be his son?"

The common people heard him gladly.

12:38 In his teaching he said to them, "Beware of the scribes, who like to walk in long robes, and to get greetings in the marketplaces, ³⁹and the best seats in the synagogues, and the best places at feasts: ⁴⁰those who devour widows' houses, and for a pretense make long prayers. These will receive greater condemnation."

12:41 Jesus sat down opposite the treasury, and saw how the multitude cast money into the treasury. Many who were rich cast in much. [42]A poor widow came, and she cast in two small brass coins, which equal a quadrans coin. [43]He called his disciples to himself, and said to them, "Most certainly I tell you, this poor widow gave more than all those who are giving into the treasury, [44]for they all gave out of their abundance, but she, out of her poverty, gave all that she had to live on."

CHAPTER THIRTEEN

¹As he went out of the temple, one of his disciples said to him, "Teacher, see what kind of stones and what kind of buildings!"

²Jesus said to him, "Do you see these great buildings? There will not be left here one stone on another, which will not be thrown down."

13:3 As HE sat on the Mount of Olives opposite the temple, Peter, James, John, and Andrew asked him privately, [4]"Tell us, when will these things be? What is the sign that these things are all about to be fulfilled?"

[5]Jesus, answering, began to tell them, "Be careful that no one leads you astray. [6]For many will come in my name, saying, 'I am he!' and will lead many astray.

[7]"When you hear of wars and rumors of wars, don't be troubled. For those must happen, but the end is not yet. [8]For nation will rise against nation, and kingdom against kingdom. There will be earthquakes in various places. There will be famines and troubles. These things are the beginning of birth pains. [9]But watch yourselves, for they will deliver you up to councils. You will be beaten in synagogues. You will stand before rulers and kings for my sake, for a testimony to them. [10]The Good News must first be preached to all the nations. [11]When they lead you away and deliver you up, don't be anxious beforehand, or premeditate what you will say, but say whatever will be given you in that hour. For it is not you who speak, but the Holy Spirit.

13:12 "BROTHER will deliver up brother to death, and the father his child. Children will rise up against parents, and cause them to be put to death. ¹³You will be hated by all men for my name's sake, but he who endures to the end will be saved. ¹⁴But when you see the abomination of desolation, spoken of by Daniel the prophet, standing where it ought not" (let the reader understand), "then let those who are in Judea flee to the mountains, ¹⁵and let him who is on the housetop not go down, nor enter in, to take anything out of his house. ¹⁶Let him who is in the field not return back to take his cloak. ¹⁷But woe to those who are with child and to those who nurse babies in those days! ¹⁸Pray that your flight won't be in the winter. ¹⁹For in those days there will be oppression, such as there has not been the like from the beginning of the creation which God created until now, and never will be. ²⁰Unless the Lord had shortened the days, no flesh would have been saved; but for the sake of the chosen ones, whom he picked out, he shortened the days. ²¹Then if anyone tells you, 'Look, here is the Christ!' or, 'Look, there!' don't believe it. ²²For there will arise false christs and false prophets, and will show signs and wonders, that they may lead astray, if possible, even the chosen ones. ²³But you watch.

13:23 "BEHOLD, I have told you all things beforehand. [24]But in those days, after that oppression, the sun will be darkened, the moon will not give its light, [25]the stars will be falling from the sky, and the powers that are in the heavens will be shaken. [26]Then they will see the Son of Man coming in clouds with great power and glory. [27]Then he will send out his angels, and will gather together his chosen ones from the four winds, from the ends of the earth to the ends of the sky.

13:28 "Now FROM the fig tree, learn this parable. When the branch has now become tender, and produces its leaves, you know that the summer is near; [29]even so you also, when you see these things coming to pass, know that it is near, at the doors. [30]Most certainly I say to you, this generation will not pass away until all these things happen. [31]Heaven and earth will pass away, but my words will not pass away. [32]But of that day or that hour no one knows, not even the angels in heaven, nor the Son, but only the Father. [33]Watch, keep alert, and pray; for you don't know when the time is.

13:34 "IT is like a man, traveling to another country, having left his house, and given authority to his servants, and to each one his work, and also commanded the door-keeper to keep watch. [35]Watch therefore, for you don't know when the lord of the house is coming, whether at evening, or at midnight, or when the rooster crows, or in the morning; [36]lest coming suddenly he might find you sleeping. [37]What I tell you, I tell all: Watch."

CHAPTER FOURTEEN

¹It was now two days before the feast of the Passover and the unleavened bread, and the chief priests and the scribes sought how they might seize him by deception, and kill him. ²For they said, "Not during the feast, because there might be a riot among the people."

³While he was at Bethany, in the house of Simon the leper, as he sat at the table, a woman came having an alabaster jar of ointment of pure nard—very costly. She broke the jar, and poured it over his head. ⁴But there were some who were indignant among themselves, saying, "Why has this ointment been wasted? ⁵For this might have been sold for more than three hundred denarii, and given to the poor." So they grumbled against her.

⁶But Jesus said, "Leave her alone. Why do you trouble her? She has done a good work for me. ⁷For you always have the poor with you, and whenever you want to, you can do them good; but you will not always have me. ⁸She has done what she could. She has anointed my body beforehand for the burying. ⁹Most certainly I tell you, wherever this Good News may be preached throughout the whole world, that which this woman has done will also be spoken of for a memorial of her."

14:10 JUDAS ISCARIOT, who was one of the twelve, went away to the chief priests, that he might deliver him to them. [11]They, when they heard it, were glad, and promised to give him money. He sought how he might conveniently deliver him.

14:12 On the first day of unleavened bread, when they sacrificed the Passover, his disciples asked him, "Where do you want us to go and prepare that you may eat the Passover?"

¹³He sent two of his disciples, and said to them, "Go into the city, and there you will meet a man carrying a pitcher of water. Follow him, ¹⁴and wherever he enters in, tell the master of the house, 'The Teacher says, "Where is the guest room, where I may eat the Passover with my disciples?"' ¹⁵He will himself show you a large upper room furnished and ready. Get ready for us there."

¹⁶His disciples went out, and came into the city, and found things as he had said to them, and they prepared the Passover.

14:17 WHEN it was evening he came with the twelve. ¹⁸As they sat and were eating, Jesus said, "Most certainly I tell you, one of you will betray me—he who eats with me."

¹⁹They began to be sorrowful, and to ask him one by one, "Surely not I?" And another said, "Surely not I?"

²⁰He answered them, "It is one of the twelve, he who dips with me in the dish. ²¹For the Son of Man goes, even as it is written about him, but woe to that man by whom the Son of Man is betrayed! It would be better for that man if he had not been born."

14:22 As they were eating, Jesus took bread, and when he had blessed, he broke it, and gave to them, and said, "Take, eat. This is my body."

²³He took the cup, and when he had given thanks, he gave to them. They all drank of it. ²⁴He said to them, "This is my blood of the new covenant, which is poured out for many. ²⁵Most certainly I tell you, I will no more drink of the fruit of the vine, until that day when I drink it anew in God's Kingdom." ²⁶When they had sung a hymn, they went out to the Mount of Olives.

14:27 Jesus said to them, "All of you will be made to stumble because of me tonight, for it is written, 'I will strike the shepherd, and the sheep will be scattered.' ²⁸However, after I am raised up, I will go before you into Galilee."

²⁹But Peter said to him, "Although all will be offended, yet I will not."

³⁰Jesus said to him, "Most certainly I tell you, that you today, even this night, before the rooster crows twice, you will deny me three times."

³¹But he spoke all the more, "If I must die with you, I will not deny you." They all said the same thing.

14:32 THEY came to a place which was named Gethsemane. He said to his disciples, "Sit here, while I pray." 33He took with him Peter, James, and John, and began to be greatly troubled and distressed. 34He said to them, "My soul is exceedingly sorrowful, even to death. Stay here, and watch."

35He went forward a little, and fell on the ground, and prayed that, if it were possible, the hour might pass away from him. 36He said, "Abba, Father, all things are possible to you. Please remove this cup from me. However, not what I desire, but what you desire."

37He came and found them sleeping, and said to Peter, "Simon, are you sleeping? Couldn't you watch one hour? 38Watch and pray, that you may not enter into temptation. The spirit indeed is willing, but the flesh is weak."

39Again he went away, and prayed, saying the same words. 40Again he returned, and found them sleeping, for their eyes were very heavy, and they didn't know what to answer him. 41He came the third time, and said to them, "Sleep on now, and take your rest. It is enough. The hour has come. Behold, the Son of Man is betrayed into the hands of sinners. 42Arise! Let's get going. Behold: he who betrays me is at hand."

14:43 IMMEDIATELY, while he was still speaking, Judas, one of the twelve, came—and with him a multitude with swords and clubs, from the chief priests, the scribes, and the elders. ⁴⁴Now he who betrayed him had given them a sign, saying, "Whomever I will kiss, that is he. Seize him, and lead him away safely." ⁴⁵When he had come, immediately he came to him, and said, "Rabbi! Rabbi!" and kissed him. ⁴⁶They laid their hands on him, and seized him. ⁴⁷But a certain one of those who stood by drew his sword, and struck the servant of the high priest, and cut off his ear.

⁴⁸Jesus answered them, "Have you come out, as against a robber, with swords and clubs to seize me? ⁴⁹I was daily with you in the temple teaching, and you didn't arrest me. But this is so that the Scriptures might be fulfilled."

14:50 THEY all left him, and fled. [51]A certain young man followed him, having a linen cloth thrown around himself over his naked body. The young men grabbed him, [52]but he left the linen cloth, and fled from them naked.

14:53 THEY led Jesus away to the high priest. All the chief priests, the elders, and the scribes came together with him.

⁵⁴Peter had followed him from a distance, until he came into the court of the high priest. He was sitting with the officers, and warming himself in the light of the fire.

14:55 Now THE chief priests and the whole council sought witnesses against Jesus to put him to death, and found none. [56]For many gave false testimony against him, and their testimony didn't agree with each other. [57]Some stood up, and gave false testimony against him, saying, [58]"We heard him say, 'I will destroy this temple that is made with hands, and in three days I will build another made without hands.'" [59]Even so, their testimony didn't agree.

[60]The high priest stood up in the middle, and asked Jesus, "Have you no answer? What is it which these testify against you?" [61]But he stayed quiet, and answered nothing. Again the high priest asked him, "Are you the Christ, the Son of the Blessed?"

[62]Jesus said, "I am. You will see the Son of Man sitting at the right hand of Power, and coming with the clouds of the sky."

[63]The high priest tore his clothes, and said, "What further need have we of witnesses? [64]You have heard the blasphemy! What do you think?" They all condemned him to be worthy of death. [65]Some began to spit on him, and to cover his face, and to beat him with fists, and to tell him, "Prophesy!" The officers struck him with the palms of their hands.

14:66 As PETER was in the courtyard below, one of the maids of the high priest came, [67]and seeing Peter warming himself, she looked at him, and said, "You were also with the Nazarene, Jesus!"

[68]But he denied it, saying, "I neither know, nor understand what you are saying." He went out on the porch, and the rooster crowed.

[69]The maid saw him, and began again to tell those who stood by, "This is one of them." [70]But he again denied it. After a little while again those who stood by said to Peter, "You truly are one of them, for you are a Galilean, and your speech shows it." [71]But he began to curse, and to swear, "I don't know this man of whom you speak!" [72]The rooster crowed the second time. Peter remembered the word, how that Jesus said to him, "Before the rooster crows twice, you will deny me three times." When he thought about that, he wept.

Chapter Fifteen

¹Immediately in the morning the chief priests, with the elders and scribes, and the whole council, held a consultation, bound Jesus, carried him away, and delivered him up to Pilate. ²Pilate asked him, "Are you the King of the Jews?"

He answered, "So you say."

³The chief priests accused him of many things. ⁴Pilate again asked him, "Have you no answer? See how many things they testify against you!"

⁵But Jesus made no further answer, so that Pilate marveled.

15:6 Now AT the feast he used to release to them one prisoner, whom they asked of him. ⁷There was one called Barabbas, bound with his fellow insurgents, men who in the insurrection had committed murder. ⁸The multitude, crying aloud, began to ask him to do as he always did for them. ⁹Pilate answered them, saying, "Do you want me to release to you the King of the Jews?" ¹⁰For he perceived that for envy the chief priests had delivered him up. ¹¹But the chief priests stirred up the multitude, that he should release Barabbas to them instead. ¹²Pilate again asked them, "What then should I do to him whom you call the King of the Jews?"

¹³They cried out again, "Crucify him!"

¹⁴Pilate said to them, "Why, what evil has he done?"

But they cried out exceedingly, "Crucify him!"

¹⁵Pilate, wishing to please the multitude, released Barabbas to them, and handed over Jesus, when he had flogged him, to be crucified.

15:16 THE soldiers led him away within the court, which is the Praetorium; and they called together the whole cohort. ¹⁷They clothed him with purple, and weaving a crown of thorns, they put it on him. ¹⁸They began to salute him, "Hail, King of the Jews!" ¹⁹They struck his head with a reed, and spat on him, and bowing their knees, did homage to him. ²⁰When they had mocked him, they took the purple off him, and put his own garments on him.

15:20 THEY led him out to crucify him. [21]They compelled one passing by, coming from the country, Simon of Cyrene, the father of Alexander and Rufus, to go with them, that he might bear his cross. [22]They brought him to the place called Golgotha, which is, being interpreted, "The place of a skull." [23]They offered him wine mixed with myrrh to drink, but he didn't take it.

15:24 CRUCIFYING HIM, they parted his garments among them, casting lots on them, what each should take. ²⁵It was the third hour, and they crucified him. ²⁶The superscription of his accusation was written over him, "THE KING OF THE JEWS." ²⁷With him they crucified two robbers; one on his right hand, and one on his left. ²⁸The Scripture was fulfilled, which says, "He was counted with transgressors."

²⁹Those who passed by blasphemed him, wagging their heads, and saying, "Ha! You who destroy the temple, and build it in three days, ³⁰save yourself, and come down from the cross!"

³¹Likewise, also the chief priests mocking among themselves with the scribes said, "He saved others. He can't save himself. ³²Let the Christ, the King of Israel, now come down from the cross, that we may see and believe him." Those who were crucified with him also insulted him.

15:33 WHEN the sixth hour had come, there was darkness over the whole land until the ninth hour. ³⁴At the ninth hour Jesus cried with a loud voice, saying, "Eloi, Eloi, lama sabachthani?" which is, being interpreted, "My God, my God, why have you forsaken me?"

³⁵Some of those who stood by, when they heard it, said, "Behold, he is calling Elijah."

³⁶One ran, and filling a sponge full of vinegar, put it on a reed, and gave it to him to drink, saying, "Let him be. Let's see whether Elijah comes to take him down."

15:37 JESUS cried out with a loud voice, and gave up the spirit. ³⁸The veil of the temple was torn in two from the top to the bottom. ³⁹When the centurion, who stood by opposite him, saw that he cried out like this and breathed his last, he said, "Truly this man was the Son of God!"

15:40 THERE were also women watching from afar, among whom were both Mary Magdalene, and Mary the mother of James the less and of Joses, and Salome; [41]who, when he was in Galilee, followed him and served him; and many other women who came up with him to Jerusalem.

15:42 WHEN evening had now come, because it was the Preparation Day, that is, the day before the Sabbath, [43]Joseph of Arimathaea, a prominent council member who also himself was looking for God's Kingdom, came. He boldly went in to Pilate, and asked for Jesus' body. [44]Pilate marveled if he were already dead; and summoning the centurion, he asked him whether he had been dead long. [45]When he found out from the centurion, he granted the body to Joseph. [46]He bought a linen cloth, and taking him down, wound him in the linen cloth, and laid him in a tomb which had been cut out of a rock. He rolled a stone against the door of the tomb. [47]Mary Magdalene and Mary, the mother of Joses, saw where he was laid.

Chapter Sixteen

[1]When the Sabbath was past, Mary Magdalene, and Mary the mother of James, and Salome, bought spices, that they might come and anoint him. [2]Very early on the first day of the week, they came to the tomb when the sun had risen. [3]They were saying among themselves, "Who will roll away the stone from the door of the tomb for us?" [4]for it was very big. Looking up, they saw that the stone was rolled back.

16:5 ENTERING into the tomb, they saw a young man sitting on the right side, dressed in a white robe, and they were amazed. ⁶He said to them, "Don't be amazed. You seek Jesus, the Nazarene, who has been crucified. He has risen. He is not here. Behold, the place where they laid him! ⁷But go, tell his disciples and Peter, 'He goes before you into Galilee. There you will see him, as he said to you.'"

16:8 THEY WENT OUT, and fled from the tomb, for trembling and astonishment had come on them. They said nothing to anyone; for they were afraid.

16:9 Now WHEN he had risen early on the first day of the week, he appeared first to Mary Magdalene, from whom he had cast out seven demons. ¹⁰She went and told those who had been with him, as they mourned and wept. ¹¹When they heard that he was alive, and had been seen by her, they disbelieved. ¹²After these things he was revealed in another form to two of them, as they walked, on their way into the country. ¹³They went away and told it to the rest. They didn't believe them, either.

16:14 AFTERWARD HE was revealed to the eleven themselves as they sat at the table, and he rebuked them for their unbelief and hardness of heart, because they didn't believe those who had seen him after he had risen. [15]He said to them, "Go into all the world, and preach the Good News to the whole creation. [16]He who believes and is baptized will be saved; but he who disbelieves will be condemned. [17]These signs will accompany those who believe: in my name they will cast out demons; they will speak with new languages; [18]they will take up serpents; and if they drink any deadly thing, it will in no way hurt them; they will lay hands on the sick, and they will recover."

16:19 SO THEN THE Lord, after he had spoken to them, was received up into heaven, and sat down at the right hand of God. ²⁰They went out, and preached everywhere, the Lord working with them, and confirming the word by the signs that followed. Amen.

ABOUT THE AUTHOR

Gary Neal Hansen, Ph.D., is the award-winning author of *Kneeling with Giants: Learning to Pray with History's Best Teachers*. An ordained Presbyterian minister, after serving as pastor of the Hillsborough Presbyterian Church in Belle Mead New Jersey he was a professor of Church history at the University of Dubuque Theological Seminary for 17 years. He now lives in Pittsburgh, Pennsylvania where he writes, speaks at retreats, consults, and teaches.

He regularly teaches courses, especially on classical spiritual disciplines such as prayer and *lectio divine*, on his website, GaryNealHansen.com.

Sign up for his newsletter there to be sure to hear about his new books and classes.

GaryNealHansen.com
Giving Christians access to their own hidden treasures.